You'll Never Get Lost Again

You'll Never Get Lost Again

Simple Navigation for Everyone

Captain Robert R. Singleton

WINCHESTER PRESS

Library of Congress Cataloging in Publication Data

Singleton, Robert R
  You'll never get lost again.

  Bibliography: p.
  1. Orientation. 2. Navigation. I. Title.
GV200.4.S64   613.6'9   79-4579
ISBN 0-87691-294-3
ISBN 0-87691-295-1 pbk.

9 8 7 6 5 4 3 2 1

Published by Winchester Press
205 East 42nd Street
New York, N. Y. 10017

WINCHESTER is a Trademark of Olin Corporation used by
Winchester Press, Inc. under authority and control of
the Trademark Proprietor
Printed in the United States of America

To Napoleon Bonaparte, Emperor of France

I dedicate this work to the great Corsican for the reason made
apparent in the following short story. I have no way of knowing
whether the story is true or not, but the idea it expresses is what's
important.

Marshal Ney, the great firebrand of France, paced back and
forth before his Emperor's desk. Napoleon seemed unim-
pressed by his first Marshal's nervous and upset condition. "Please
hear me," Ney pleaded. Napoleon studied a map of Russia with a
jaundiced eye.

"My dear Ney, calm yourself."

"But, Emperor, this man DeFarge whom you have made a general is the dumbest man in all of France."

"Yes, isn't it wonderful?"

"But, but this man is a joke, a baboon, a turkey."

"Yes," agreed Napoleon calmly, "it took us years to find such a
man. We searched the country over and he was carefully chosen."

"But, Worship, you have made him a full general on your staff
and he's an idiot."

"I agree," said Napoleon. "He is an idiot, but he is also one of
the most important men in my Empire."

"But why?" asked Ney, completely baffled. "Why?"

The Emperor waited a long silent moment for his Marshal to
regain his composure. "When I give an order," he said, at last, "I
always give it in the presence of this man DeFarge. I state my orders
simply so that DeFarge can understand them. And if DeFarge can
understand my instructions, there is no excuse for anyone else not
to."

Well, we all know what happened. Napoleon was exiled. Ney
was executed. As for DeFarge, legend has it that he somehow es-
caped to America, married, changed his name, and fathered fifteen
children whose descendants are involved in politics to this very day.

Contents

CHAPTER ONE: **Understanding Navigation and Direction**   **1**

    The Direction Circle   5

CHAPTER TWO: **The Magnetic Compass**   **9**

CHAPTER THREE: **Compass Variation**   **19**

    Compass Variation Exercise   24

CHAPTER FOUR: **Let's Navigate**   **27**

    Exercise No. 1   There and Back   28

    Exercise No. 2   Around the Block or Backyard   30

    Exercise No. 3   The Treasure Map   34

    Exercise No. 4   Navigating Away from Civilization   37

    Exercise No. 5   Estimating a Direction   46

CHAPTER FIVE: **Cross-country Navigation**   **50**

    Understanding Dead Reckoning   57

    Planning the Cross-country Trip   64

CHAPTER SIX: **Safety in the Field**   **73**

    Preparation   74

    Equipment List   74

    Lost   76

    Getting Out Without Compass or Map   80

    Traveling at Night Without a Compass   83

CHAPTER SEVEN: **Navigation for the Boatman**   **89**

    The Nautical Chart   91

    Aids to Navigation   95

    Plotting on the Nautical Chart—Steps 1 through 5   100

    Electronic Navigation Aids   104

Further Reading   **109**

Navigation Notebook   **111**

Index   **117**

You'll Never Get
Lost Again

CHAPTER

1

Understanding Navigation and Direction

Stated simply, navigation is the science of getting yourself or your vehicle from one place to another. Here's an example of how the science works:

Get out of your chair, go into the kitchen, get a beer or what have you, and return to your chair.

No matter how simple this sounds, you have navigated and performed several automatic actions on your outward and return trips.

1. You chose a destination.
2. You followed *reference points* to that destination.
3. You traveled at a certain speed.
4. It took you a specific length of time to reach your destination. Once you were there, you reversed direction and returned to your original starting point.

Now let's look at the factors involved:

• Objective • Direction • Distance • Speed • Time

All these factors are involved whenever we move from one place to another, whether it's to the refrigerator or across the ocean or to the corner grocery store.

Let's have a look at the path you traveled to the kitchen.

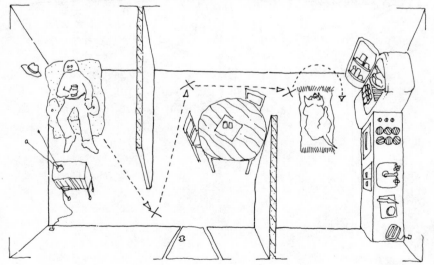

Understanding Navigation and Direction

You can see by the path line that you changed your direction three times because of obstacles in your way. Had there been no obstacles your path line would have looked like this:

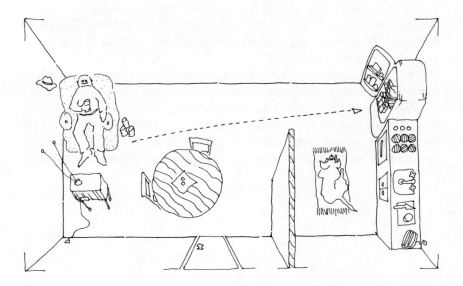

Your distance would have been less and assuming you used the same speed as before your traveling time would have been shorter.

Now let's look at those obstacles. You were familiar with each one and each was a reference point that you used on your journey to your objective.

This is the simplest form of navigation: following one known reference point to another until you reach your destination. We spend all our lives doing this. It is when we lose sight of an objective and have no familiar reference points to guide us that we lose direction, or, in other words, we get lost.

There are many devices available today that we can use as aids to navigation. Some are simple—almost foolproof—and easy to understand, while others are extremely complicated and are used mainly by professionals. Later, we will touch briefly on the complicated aids and explain their functions.

However, in my 20 years as a boat driver, airplane pilot, and backwoods brush buster, I have found that the simple aids are usually best. In several cases I know of, the more complicated method or instrument failed. It was the easy-to-use old stand-by that got the person back to the barn. So, it's the simple methods and tools that we will cover in detail.

Not too long ago, during an introduction to a course in Basic Navigation I teach, one of my students at Hampshire College in Amherst, Massachusetts, asked the question, "What is the most important tool in navigation?"

I put the question back to the class and the answer was quick in coming from a young Nova Scotian whose family spend their lives at sea. "Common sense," he said, smiling. And, without a doubt, he was right. It has been my experience, after several hundred search and rescue operations at sea, to find after talking to the people involved that common sense is the most neglected tool of all.

The Direction Circle

We're going to have to get you out of your chair again. Stand up and face an object, let's say your mother-in-law's picture on the wall. Now, slowly turn yourself in a complete circle, stopping where you started. You have just faced 360 different directions in which you could have traveled, provided there were no barriers or obstacles in your way.

No matter where you are or what's around you, you always have those 360 directions, or degrees, to choose from. And, remember, even as you move, you still have a circle measuring 360 degrees around you.

The top of this circle, at the 360 and zero mark, we'll label North. The very bottom, at the 180-degree mark, we'll mark South. And on the right-hand side, exactly at the 90-degree mark, is East. Its opposite, on the left-hand side at 270 degrees, is West.

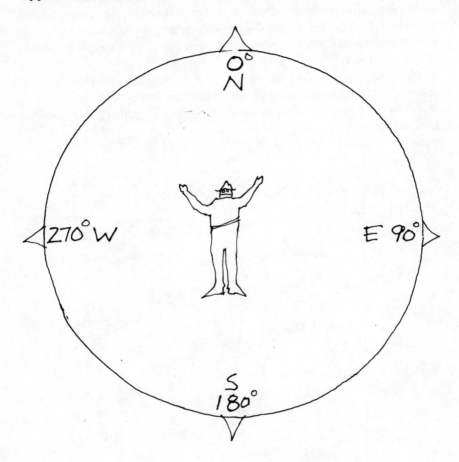

Understanding Navigation and Direction

These are the four major directions; North is the most important, and you'll see why soon.

Now let's look at the 45-degree mark between North and East. Label it Northeast. (Doesn't that bring back memories of old sea movies? "Bring her to the Nor'east, Mr. Christian.")

Now it should be easy for you to locate Southeast, Southwest, and Northwest there at the 135-, 225-, and 315-degree marks.

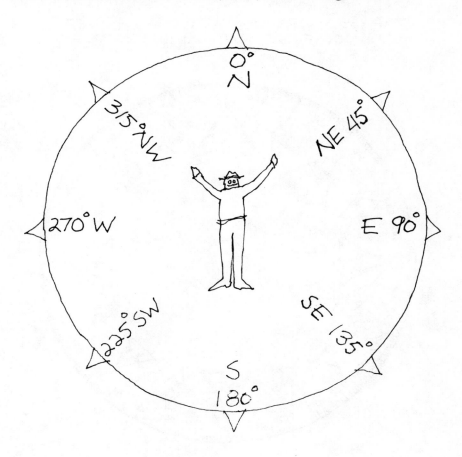

What we have done so far is to label degrees as directions. We can do this further by splitting the difference between the ones we have now. In this way, you can now locate North Northeast, and North Northwest, and so on. When we start cutting directions any finer, I prefer to use numerical degree designations instead. That way there is less chance of making a mistake.

COMPASS CARD SHOWING ALL POINTS
OF COMPASS AND ALL DEGREES

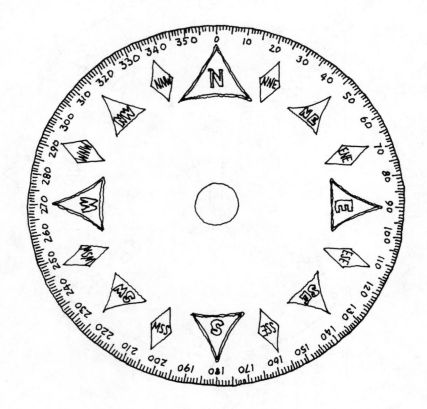

Understanding Navigation and Direction

2

The Magnetic Compass

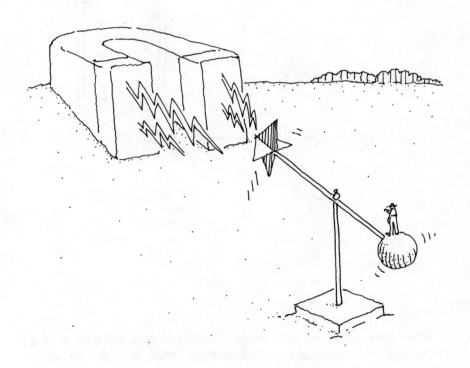

Now that you have an understanding of degrees and the directions they represent, let's go back to that picture on the wall that we used as a beginning point. It gave us a point at which to start the beginning of our circle.

Remember what we said about always being in the middle of a circle with 360 directions to choose from. Well, in order for us to keep the directions in the same place, no matter where we move, we need a mark or beginning point that will not change.

This is what a *magnetic compass* has: it always points North, and it is this factor which makes North so important. A magnetic compass is a small magnetized needle or wheel that is attracted to a large

The Magnetic Compass

magnetic deposit near the North Pole. Of all the tools used in navigation, the magnetic compass is the simplest, and one of the most important ever developed by man.

The average hand-held magnetic compass consists of a magnetized needle, a *compass card* (a circle with the degrees and directions on it, which you are familiar with by now), a post, and a case made of nonmagnetic material.

The needle is suspended from the center post and swings free enabling it to find North. This swinging motion is called *homing*. Most well made, hand-held compasses, and the majority of marine compasses, are liquid-filled, with either an alcohol or mineral oil solution, which helps slow the homing action and steadies the needle for easier reading.

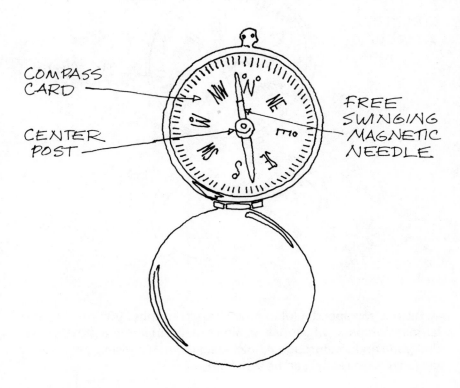

THE MAGNETIC COMPASS

COMPASS CARD

CENTER POST

FREE SWINGING MAGNETIC NEEDLE

The *marine compass* is a little different in construction, but it still performs the same function of showing you in which direction magnetic North lies.

If you haven't already purchased a compass, you should do so at once before planning a trip. You will find them at varying prices from $1.50 and upwards, but $4.00 to $8.00 should buy a pretty good instrument. I paid $3.50 for mine, but that was when gas was 28¢ a gallon.

Try to find one with a *direction arrow;* that's a small needle that you can set to any degree that you want to remember or follow.

MARINE COMPASS

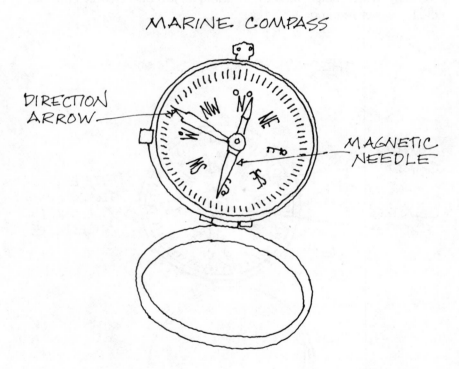

DIRECTION ARROW

MAGNETIC NEEDLE

Also, if you spend a lot of time in open country, you may want a *lensatic compass,* which has an attachment similar to a gun sight so that you can look through it, take a sighting on a distant object and get a direction reading at the same time.

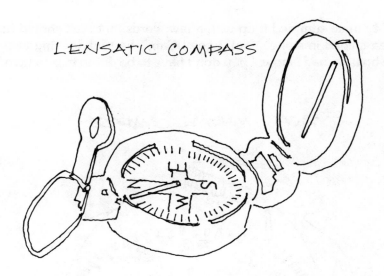

LENSATIC COMPASS

If you own a boat and plan to spend a lot of time on the water, there is no substitute for a good dependable marine compass, and you should be prepared to spend a few extra dollars to buy a really good one. Your own life and the lives of your family and friends, not to mention the survival of both boat and equipment, may depend on it.

However, the most expensive compass in existence isn't worth a damn if you don't know how to read it.

During the summer of 1972, while bass fishing in Cape Cod Bay, I received a radio call to be on the lookout for a 26-foot sailboat that had been missing for a little over 2 days. As fortune would have it, we located this boat about 15 miles out. Its two occupants were sun-burned, thirsty, and half starved. They had sailed into the Bay from Boston and when they lost sight of land, due to thick haze, they lost all sense of direction.

After making sure they were all right, I asked what had been the problem. They said the compass didn't work; somehow it wasn't reading correctly. My mate and I inspected the instrument and found it was one of the most expensive models available. It was in perfect working order.

After questioning the two men further, we found both to be high-level professionals in their respective fields.

The Magnetic Compass

My mate summed it up with a few words that I felt should have been etched in stone. "You know, Cap," he said, looking back at the boat we had in tow, "you don't have to be dumb to be stupid."

TYPICAL MARINE COMPASS

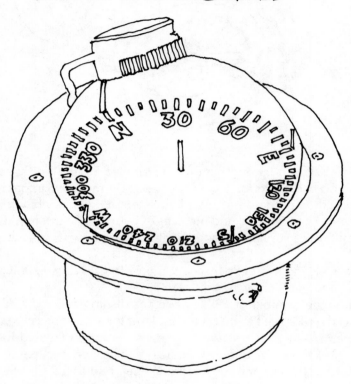

The Magnetic Compass

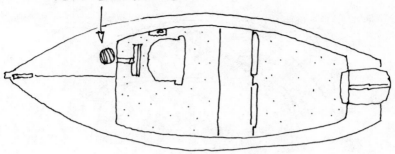

USUAL MOUNTING LOCATION FOR SMALL BOAT

Other types of compasses that are in use today are electric driven, gyro-operated, and are used primarily in large ships. Their cost would stagger your imagination.

All commercial aircraft also carry *gyro compasses,* and so do most private planes. Their cost isn't quite as high as the large ship's instruments, but it would go a long way toward paying a family's food bill for the year.

In most cases where these instruments are used in ships or airplanes, an inexpensive simple magnetic compass is used as a back-up.

TYPICAL AIRCRAFT COMPASS

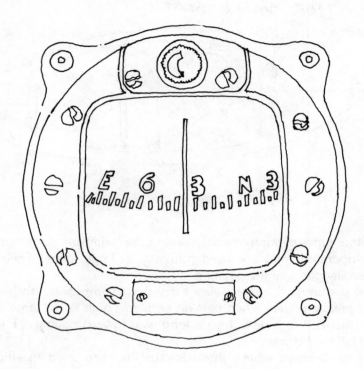

USUAL MOUNTING LOCATION
FOR AIRPLANE

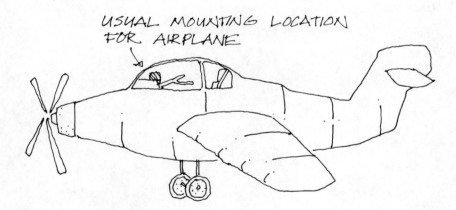

The Magnetic Compass

SHIPS MAGNETIC COMPASS

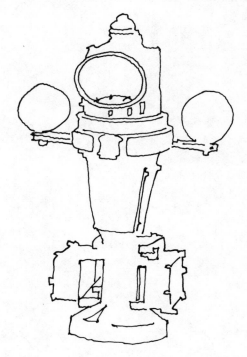

SHIPS GYRO COMPASS

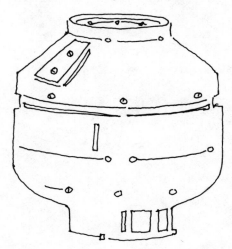

CHAPTER
3
Compass Variation

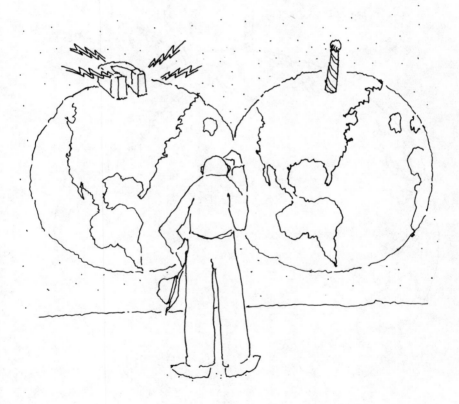

Well, now you've done it. You went out and bought yourself a shiny new compass, or maybe you borrowed one from that nice scout next door. But, just hold it for a minute before you head for the Klondike or search for the lost treasures of El Dorado. There are a few more details you should know about.

First of all, there's *compass variation*. Remember, earlier I said a magnetic compass points toward a magnetic deposit? Well, that's right, but the *magnetic North Pole* is not in the same place as the *true North Pole* as you will see in the following illustration.

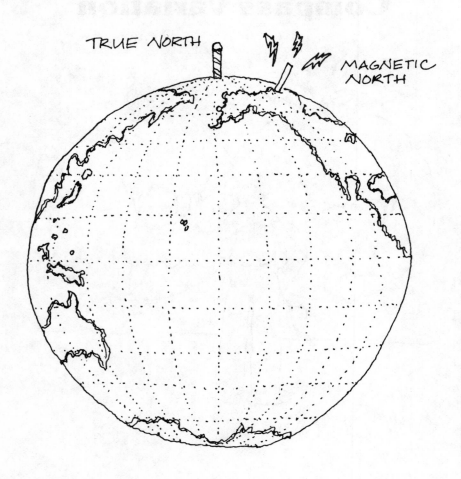

Compass Variation

Actually, the Earth's magnetic field moves in somewhat erratic lines (called *Isogonic* lines) across the surface of the globe. Very few of these isogonic lines point true North.

In order for you to determine what the compass variation is in your area, you may want to purchase a U.S. Geological *survey map*, a *coastal chart*, or an *aviation map* for this information, or see the next illustration for an approximate idea.

Compass variation can be either East or West of true North. For example: let's say you are a New Englander and you have a 15 degree westerly variation. That means if your compass needle is on zero degrees magnetic North, true North will read as 15 degrees magnetic.

If you live in the central United States, you may not have a compass variation at all. Magnetic North and true North are likely to be the same.

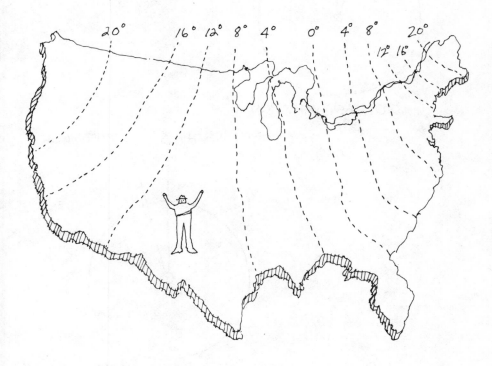

Those of you living in the western states will have an easterly variation. Example: If there is a 20 degree easterly variation in your area and the compass is aligned to magnetic North, then true North is 340 degrees magnetic.

The old rule is *East is least; West is best.* To put it more simply, when converting from magnetic North to true North, add for West variations, subtract for East variation.

20° EAST VARIATION

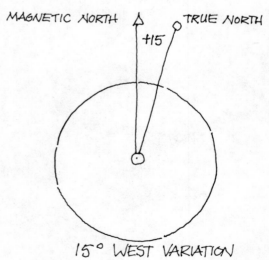

15° WEST VARIATION

Compass Variation

EAST VARIATION
SUBTRACT
FROM
TRUE

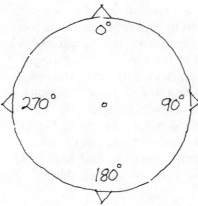

WESTERN U.S.
HAS
EASTERLY
VARIATIONS

EASTERN U.S.
HAS
WESTERLY
VARIATIONS

0°

270°   °   90°

180°

WEST VARIATION
ADD
TO
TRUE

Compass Variation

Compass Variation Exercise

1. You're walking 45° magnetic. What is your true heading if you have a 10° west variation? **A. 55°**
2. At 320° true with a 15° East variation, what is your magnetic course? **A. 305°**
3. At 20° East variation, what is the true heading of a magnetic course of 135°? **A. 115°**
4. At 12° West variation, what direction would you be going if you were walking 348° magnetic? **A. true north**

You must remember that variation is the angle between magnetic and true North, and that variation changes with location.

At this point, let me remind you that in simple navigation there is little need to convert to true readings. However, a basic knowledge of true readings is necessary, as you will see in later chapters when we begin to work with the topographical map.

There are other factors that affect the magnetic compass; most important is *compass error.* To see this factor at work, place your new compass on a table in front of you. Let the needle settle and turn the compass to align with magnetic North. Now go get a hammer or screwdriver or something made out of cast iron or steel and move it around your compass and watch what happens to the needle. Notice how it moves toward the metal object you're holding.

This action doesn't mean your compass is defective. It just shows you that a compass can be attracted to other forces as well as to the Earth's magnetic field. An electric current from a nearby wire will drive that little needle crazy.

If you ever have to install a compass in your car, boat, snowmobile, or one of the many other recreational vehicles now in use, you will undoubtedly have to correct the compass. Try to mount it as far away as possible from steel and sources of electricity.

Most compass manufacturers supply instructions and diagrams for correcting the compass. However, the most important factor is to make sure that the vehicle is pointing in a North-South direction before you adjust the instrument. You can do this by using your hand-held compass, but make sure you are away from the vehicle when you take a reading.

One easy method I used when installing a compass in my pick-up truck was this: I drove out to an empty supermarket parking lot with my two children one Sunday. I took a reading and had the children place plastic garbage pails at North and South headings. I then lined up the truck exactly between the two pails and adjusted the compass. It was when we were doing the East-West adjustments that the police showed up. I had a little explaining to do after my daughter informed the officer that he had to move his car because he was creating a *magnetic interference* for her father.

When making adjustments on a mounted compass, you must always remember to use a brass or bronze screwdriver. If you don't have one, you can make one by filing down the end of a piece of brass welding rod.

While we're on the subject of compass interference I'll tell you a story about a certain friend of mine, a third-generation lobster fisherman with over 40 years experience at sea. It was during our "monsoon" season, when weather systems pass over the Cape on an almost hourly basis.

What had been a sparkling blue morning quickly turned into rain and black fog. My friend had taken a sighting on a string of his lobster pots when the thick fog rolled in. Normally, there's nothing to worry about. He had the compass course memorized and it would be just a couple of minutes and he would be in his pot line. Well, the couple of minutes turned into five, and the five into ten. My friend turned his vessel around and supposedly retraced his path for 15 minutes. No pot line.

At this point he was in the process of inventing a new language, when he discovered that a well-meaning relative had left a galvanized bucket full of eight-penny nails and a hammer aboard the boat.

They had been repairing a beach house on a nearby peninsula and had forgotten to take the bucket off the boat. This in itself was not bad, but my friend's relative had placed the bucket on a shelf inside the cabin about 10 inches away from the bottom of the compass housing.

When he was telling me the story he figured that with the compass error induced by the bucket, if he had stayed "on course" he would have reached Iceland in 6 days.

There are other factors that influence the magnetic compass but most of these occur in aircraft-mounted instruments and where speed is involved. I feel their explanation is not needed here as they are not crucial to simple navigation. However, for those of you who want to learn more on the subject, a list of excellent books will be given at the end of this volume.

CHAPTER
4
Let's Navigate

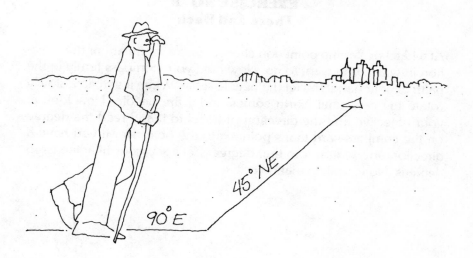

This chapter will teach you to use the compass in the field. Before you set out, make sure you have a pencil, a small pad or notebook, and a watch. A comfortable pair of walking shoes will come in handy, too.

"But, I live in the city," you may say. Don't worry, you'll have just as much fun as your country cousin. Besides, when someone asks you what you're doing, you can impress the hell out of him by sticking out your chin and pointing along your direction of travel and exclaiming that you're following a *magnetic bearing* of such and such degrees. You can imagine what he will think!

EXERCISE NO. 1
There and Back

At whatever starting point you choose, face a landmark or the direction in which you want to go. Now hold your compass firmly in the palm of your hand and let the needle settle. When it's steady, slowly rotate the case until North comes under the needle. Now look at your objective and the direction of travel to it and read the degree on the compass card that's pointing to the objective. If you have a direction arrow, turn it to that degree. Let's say your heading is 45 degrees. Now, walk to that objective.

A   TO ————⟶°   B

⟵————° RETURN

Let's Navigate

Easy, isn't it? Just for practice, read your compass and turn your direction arrow to the return heading 225 degrees and go back to your starting point, only this time look at your watch and time yourself.

Let's say it took you 5 minutes to return, walking at the same pace. You now know that to get from your starting point (Point A) to your objective (Point B), you will follow a direction of 45 degrees for five minutes. To return it's 5 minutes at 225 degrees.

Should a thick fog limit your vision, you would still be able to get there by frequently checking your compass.

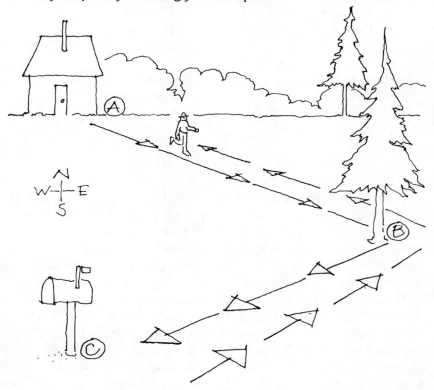

Using your own compass, indicate where magnetic North is on "A." Then pencil in the degrees and name of directions you traveled.

Beginning at "A" what would be the degrees and directions that represent to and from "C."

EXERCISE NO. 2
Around the Block or Backyard

This time go around the block and write down each change of direction in your notebook, along with the time it took you to reach each point. You may want to draw a diagram to this exercise so as to help you understand the factor involved, or you can just fill in the blank spaces on the following illustration, after using your compass.

A to B
Direction _____
Degrees _____
Time _____

C to D
Direction _____
Degrees _____
Time _____

B to C
Direction _____
Degrees _____
Time _____

D to A
Direction _____
Degrees _____
Time _____

Did you have a nice walk? Now, write down the reverse headings of your trip, and draw a map of your walk. Perhaps it wasn't exactly square like the one in the diagram. At each direction change, draw a small circle and indicate magnetic North with an arrow. Then, as best you can, give an approximate direction from B to D and A to C and their return headings.

Before going on to the next exercise, it might be a good idea to figure out how fast you move. An average person can walk a mile in 15 minutes or 4 miles an hour. Those of you who jog will probably cut this time in half. If you are a hunter or in the backwoods, your pace over broken ground will average about 2 miles an hour. Don't forget to take into consideration the type of terrain involved. Remember, you'll usually go downhill a lot faster than you'll go up.

Another thing you'll want to remember while you're practicing navigation is to take note of the position of the sun (if it's visible, of course). At each direction change, make a note as to the date and time of day and where the sun is from the direction you're walking.

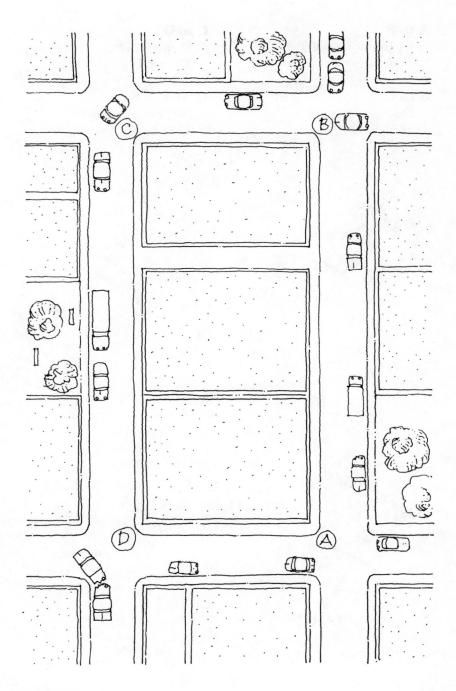

A to B

    Degrees of travel   _____

    Time to B   _____

C to D

    Degrees of travel   _____

    Time to D   _____

B to C

    Degrees of travel   _____

    Time to C   _____

D to A

    Degrees of travel   _____

    Time to A   _____

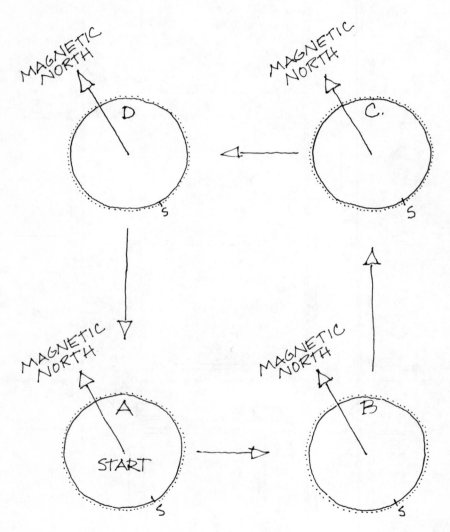

Let's Navigate

This serves two purposes. It will teach you how to judge a direction without a compass, and it will give you a guide mark while following a magnetic heading.

For example, if it's early in the morning and you're walking 90 degrees and the sun is directly in your face, you won't need a compass to know you're walking East. By putting the rising sun on your right shoulder, you'll be facing North. Familiarity with this fact will come in handy should you lose your compass while in the field.

EXERCISE NO. 3
The Treasure Map

This exercise is meant for two or more people and can be a lot of fun for all concerned.

First of all, you'll need something to bury or hide, like a six-pack of beer or a bottle of rum—something that everyone will enjoy when it is found.

Now, starting from a given place, take a reading and time the distance between direction changes. The more detailed and intricate you make the map, the more fun everyone has, especially if they have to crawl and climb over things to reach an objective. Instead of timing the distance between the last few direction changes, count the paces. Your friends will really love you if you find a nice swamp for them to wade through. Don't draw a map like the ones you see in pirate movies, just write down compass headings and time or places.

EXAMPLE: Starting at the back door of Joe's Bar and Grill.

95°	11 minutes
60°	9 minutes
260°	8½ minutes
20°	till you reach a stone wall
180°	3½ minutes till you reach a large oak, then 15 paces at
140°	X marks the spot.

You can double the fun by making another map with different readings, but both going to the same place. This means two or more teams can compete for the prize.

I'm sure you can be a little more imaginative in your map-making than I have been. However, don't forget to tell your friends that this type of exercise in navigation is definitely not a black tie affair. Cross-country skiers and snowmobilers can play a form of this game, only everyone meets at the "X" for a cookout.

Write the compass headings and time yourself to your nearest grocery store. Use the space below to draw a map of your trip. Then as best you can, determine what would have been the direct heading to your objective, providing that there were no obstacles in your way.

N

W   **E**

S

What general direction would you walk to return to base in the shortest possible time; assuming you have followed a compass heading of 10° for 20 minutes, then changed direction to 70° for an additional 20 minutes? Use the space below to draw a diagram of this problem.

N

W   **E**

S

EXERCISE NO. 4
Navigating Away from Civilization

This exercise is for people who spend time in the mountains and forest or open country and make a habit of venturing into unfamiliar places. With the possible exception of the weekend boater, hunters, weekend explorers, and cross-country skiers are more apt to get lost than any other group. We'll cover the particular problems of the weekend boater in a later chapter.

By now you should be adept at using your compass and taking a reading. As you have seen, it's a very reliable instrument as long as you use it correctly. During this exercise, I hope to teach you always to trust it.

There have been times in my life when I could have sworn the darn thing was lying or not operating properly. I have been absolutely positive I was going in the right direction and the compass was very persistent in letting me know I was wrong. In all of these disagreements, the compass won.

I know of no hunter or outdoorsman who hasn't doubted his compass at one time or another. So, when it happens to you, don't feel lonesome; others have been there before you. Always make sure there is nothing to influence the compass while you're taking a reading.

If you're hunting, lean your rifle against a tree and step away a pace or so. That 9 pounds of steel held too close can send you off to rediscover North America if you're not careful. Another good idea is to tie the compass to your belt so you won't lose it. I use a 15-inch piece of rawhide with a large loop in one end to slip around my belt. That way if it should fall out of my pocket it won't go anywhere.

A close friend of mine, a man I've hunted deer with since I was a boy, tells the story of having lost his compass while hunting in a wilderness area of northern Vermont. It was snowing and there were no familiar landmarks. As he said, it all looked the same. He sat down to reason the situation out when he discovered the compass had fallen through a hole in the side of his pocket and down into his hunting pants, which luckily were tucked into his boots. He was wearing long johns and couldn't feel the compass against his leg as he walked.

Now, let's get back to our exercise. First of all, find an area whose roads you're familiar with. My best recommendation is a backcountry dirt road with forest on both sides. Park your vehicle and get away from it before using your compass. Find out which way the road travels and jot it down in your notebook. Draw a line to represent the road. Next, choose a direction directly away from the road and find its opposite reading. Don't forget to jot that down too, or your friends may never see you again. Let's say the road runs North and South and you plan to hunt or explore the West side of it. Your notebook information should look like this.

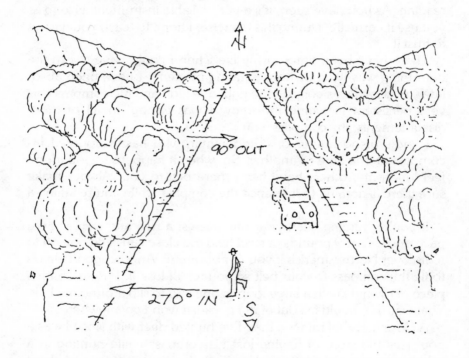

Use this space for drawing your own map.

N

W

E

S

Now you know that no matter where you go on the West side of the road you won't be lost. When it comes time to leave, all you do is walk East and you'll come out somewhere on the road your car is parked on.

In order to give yourself confidence while you're in the field, put your compass away and spend a few minutes getting lost. Wander around a little and don't worry about the situation. It's kind of nice being away from the world for awhile. When you're ready to go, that compass will guide you out.

The following illustration will help you understand this exercise.

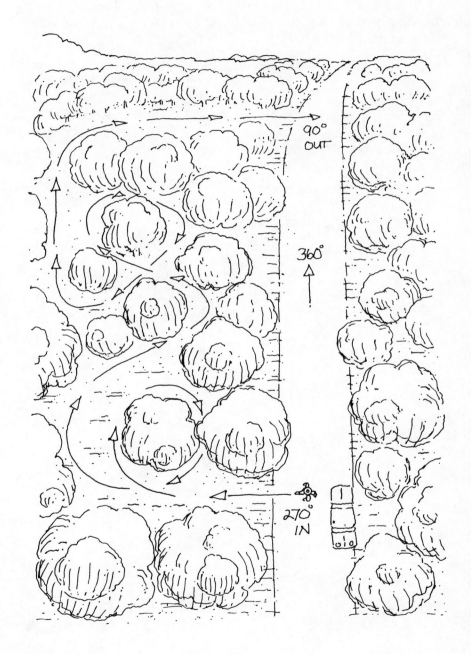

90°
OUT

360°

270°
IN

You are at X and plan to explore the right-hand side of this road. In what general direction would you be walking and what would your return direction be?

You are at X and plan to walk a northerly direction into the forest. What direction would get you back to the road other than South? Let's assume it's 4:00 pm and you followed this direction. Where would the sun be in relation to your line of travel?

Let's assume you've lost your compass and you're at X. It's 10:00 am on a clear morning. What general direction would you walk to get to the road? Also, what would be the most direct direction to your car?

If you noticed, in this exercise we made no mention of keeping time. The reason is that for the most part there was no need to do so. The important thing was to learn to trust the compass and plan your direction before you started out. Most hikers and hunters I know use time in a general sense only. They estimate how long they have walked and how long it will take to get back. You may want to time yourself on your first few trips into the field, and it won't hurt, but knowing in what direction to travel is most important.

There is one rule you may want to remember when in an unfamiliar area: *Always know where you are 2 hours before sundown.*

A. West Northwest;

EXERCISE NO. 5
Estimating a Direction

This exercise is similar to the preceding one, only this time instead of wandering around, take a heading and parallel the road you're parked on—let's say 15 to 20 minutes of walking. Now, instead of taking your return heading out to the road, try to estimate what direction will take you out nearest your car.

You just might surprise yourself and hit it right on the nose. And, if not, I'll bet you come close. Also, you will find that this will teach you to save time by using the shortest distance. Another point to remember as you grow more confident in this: Always choose a reference point you can't miss. A long road, a river or stream, or a large open field is excellent. Never choose anything too small or indistinct or you might walk past it.

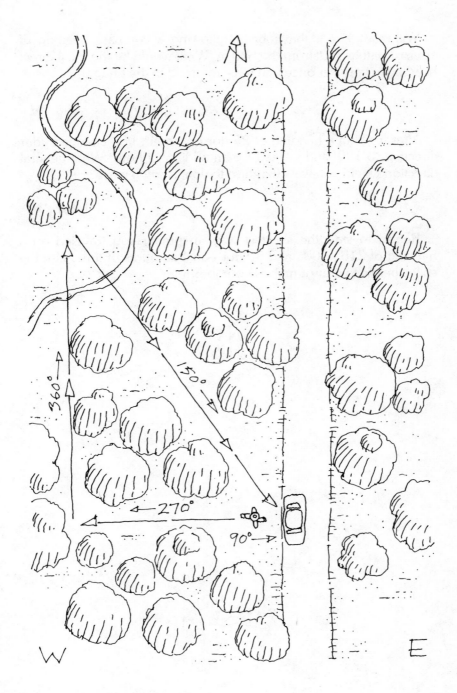

You're at X and have been following a compass heading of approximately 310° from the bridge. What would be the most direct heading to your car once you have returned to the bridge?

A. 250°

After walking a heading of 25° for one hour, you changed your direction to 130° and walked for an additional hour. What general direction would you walk to return to your starting place?

A. West

Return to start the shortest way, assuming you traveled on a heading of 215°, 300°, and 40° for equal amounts of time. Use the space below to draw a map of your journey.

5

Cross-country Navigation

Cross-country navigation is the most advanced form of simple navigation that you can undertake. Above all, you'll need careful planning and confidence in yourself and to understand the use of some other tools besides your compass. The preceding exercises have taught you the basic principles of simple navigation. In cross-country work you put them all to use in traveling over distances through wilderness or in completely unfamiliar surroundings to reach your objective.

Other than common sense and a good compass, the third most useful navigation aid you can have is a U.S. Geological Survey map of the area that you're going to. These maps can be purchased in sporting-goods stores and bookstores, or you can write to the U.S. Geological Survey, Washington, D.C. 20242.

They are generally known as *topographical maps* or topo maps, for short, each of which covers the area of about a seven-mile square. Whichever term you choose to use will be correct. Should you decide to write to Washington, it would be advisable to have them send you a booklet explaining all the chart symbols used on the map, because we will only be covering the most important ones in this text.

Cross-country Navigation

If you have never seen one of these maps, you'll find the first glance an interesting and almost frightening experience. All those thousands of little lines running all over the place, why it's enough to make a grown man cry, you say. The lines are called *contour lines* and they have a story to tell. Just suppose you are in an aircraft over mountainous country and you are looking straight down. What will you see? At first glance the country will look flat or nearly so. It's only when you look at those mountains from an angle that you get an idea of their shape and size.

Cross-country Navigation

Map makers use the lines to show us the shape of the land, while giving us a vertical view of it. Unless otherwise stated on your map, contour lines are shown at 20-foot intervals. The closer the lines come together, the steeper the grade. The following illustration will show you what I mean.

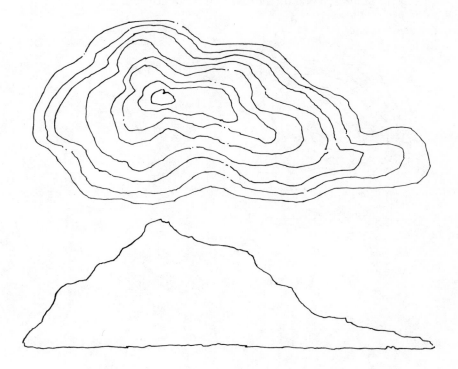

Looking a little closer at the contour lines you'll notice that every fifth line is printed a little heavier and darker than its neighbors. These are the 100-foot intervals and are quite helpful in measuring short distances. If you see those 100 lines close together, you can bet the piece of ground is almost vertical. Flat terrain with little change in elevation will be almost devoid of contour lines.

Cross-country Navigation

The height of most prominent hills or mountains on your course will be given in feet above sea level, and will be printed near the summit. If the elevation of a particular mound or hill that you're interested in isn't given, then it's a simple matter to count contour lines and multiply by 20 for your answer.

Suppose you're in the field and you're looking at a hill with a given elevation of 1000 feet and it appears to you to be only half that height. Remember that the plain or flat ground that you're standing on may be 500 feet above sea level and the hill is on that plain. What you have is a 500-foot hill setting on a flat plain that's 500 feet above sea level.

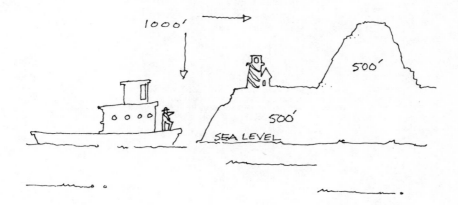

Geological survey maps are extremely accurate as far as positioning, contour, and elevation are concerned, and credit should be given to those geologists, surveyors, and pilots who developed them. However, for roads and highways and trails, it's another matter. It's not that the ones marked on the map are in the wrong place, but that most of the geological survey maps were made in the late 1920s and our country and its network of highways, roads, and trails have gone through a lot of changes since then.

So, never use a survey map as a road map because a survey map is a picture of the land as it appeared to the map makers as long ago as the 1920s. Elevation and slope probably won't have changed much, but everything else will have changed a great deal.

Cross-country Navigation

At the bottom of a survey map you'll find a set of scales, one in miles, another in kilometers, and another in feet. By using a straightedge, you can measure the distance between two points quite accurately. I am a little old-fashioned and still prefer miles to kilometers, but you can use whatever unit of measurement you find most convenient.

At the bottom of your map you will also find two arrows. One points toward true North, the other to magnetic North, and between them is the degree of variation from magnetic to true for the area covered by that map.

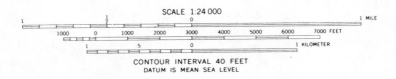

SCALE 1:24 000

CONTOUR INTERVAL 40 FEET
DATUM IS MEAN SEA LEVEL

THIS MAP COMPLIES WITH NATIONAL MAP ACCURACY STANDARDS
FOR SALE BY U. S. GEOLOGICAL SURVEY, WASHINGTON, D. C. 20242
A FOLDER DESCRIBING TOPOGRAPHIC MAPS AND SYMBOLS IS AVAILABLE ON REQUEST

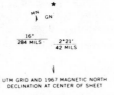

UTM GRID AND 1967 MAGNETIC NORTH
DECLINATION AT CENTER OF SHEET

In the field, always make sure the survey map points true North. To do this, first find the magnetic North; then use the direction arrow to indicate the true North heading. Now, set the map down facing true North. In case you haven't already noticed, the map has longitude and latitude lines. Longitudes run North and South, latitudes East and West. Let's assume you're about to set out on a cross-country trip from a point that you have located on your map. Hold your compasss directly over the map and turn the map until the longitude lines are pointing in the same direction as the direction arrow pointing to true North. When the map is lined up, step back and look around. Usually, about this time, you really begin to appreciate the work and precision that went into making these maps so long ago.

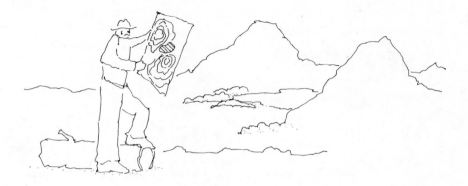

Understanding Dead Reckoning

Of all the terms used in navigation, *dead reckoning* is the least understood, yet probably the easiest to explain. In a movie about Charles Lindbergh's epic solo flight across the Atlantic, Jimmy Stewart says the only thing wrong with dead reckoning is the word dead. I agree. This term somehow evolved from the term *deduced reckoning,* which came from an era when ships were wood and the men who sailed in them were supposedly iron.

Dead reckoning is a method of approximating your position by knowing how much ground you covered in a certain amount of time from a known position. Remember, in an earlier exercise, I asked you to time yourself and to find out approximately how fast you traveled over different types of terrain. That information is the basis for determining a dead reckoning position. By knowing how fast you travel and how long you have traveled, you can estimate how far you have traveled. Should you be following a compass course outlined on your survey map, you will be able to determine your position.

For example, let's say you left Joe's Bar and Grill at twelve noon and you are traveling 2 miles per hour on a compass course of 270 degrees. The terrain is flat forest country, and you have very few

landmarks to help you find your position. At the end of 2 hours, you want to see approximately where you are on the map. You know that after 2 hours you have traveled 4 miles.

Take a straightedge and measure the mileage scale at the bottom of the map; then place it along your direction of travel from Joe's Bar and Grill. Pencil in an "X" at 4 miles. That's your dead reckoning position. If you haven't deviated from course and have taken into consideration the time spent resting, you will have a fairly accurate idea of your position, and you will be able to estimate your time of arrival at your objective.

Always remember this: A dead reckoning position is an estimated position. Nothing takes the place of physical, recognizable landmarks on your map, and they, above all, should be used as checkpoints when possible.

The term dead reckoning, when used in reference to navigation at sea, is a method of estimating a ship's location between positions that, in most cases, are out of sight of land and that have been determined by use of celestial navigation instruments. The methods and equipment used are a bit more sophisticated, but the basic principle is the same.

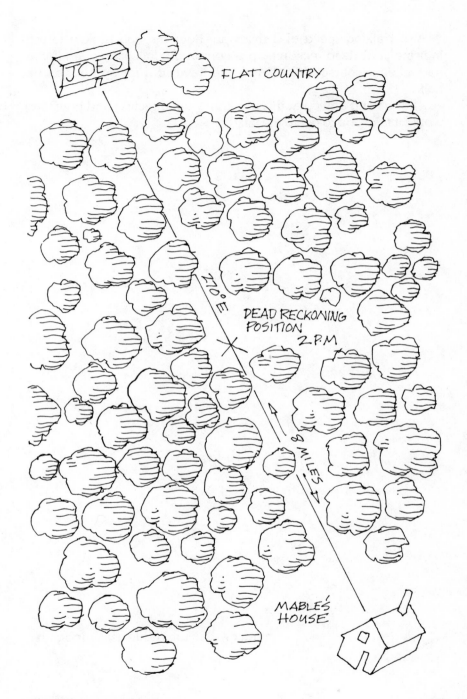

JOE'S

FLAT COUNTRY

210° E

DEAD RECKONING
POSITION
2 P.M

8 MILES

MABLE'S
HOUSE

At a walking speed of 2 miles per hour through broken forest, indicate your dead reckoning position on the following map, if you had taken a course of 290° and had traveled it for an hour and a half.

After having arrived at this position, what direction and how long would it take you to get to the lake?

A. Southwest; approximately 45 minutes

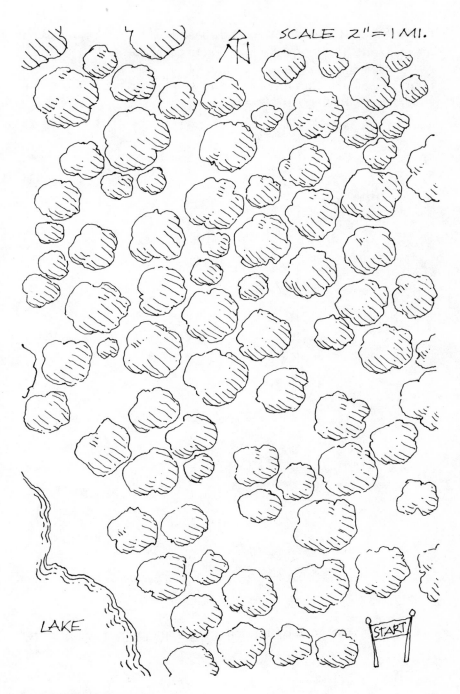

SCALE 2"=1 MI.

LAKE

START

You are at X and your traveling speed is 2 miles per hour. What direction and how long will it take you to get to Joe's Bar and Grill?

After leaving Joe's on a heading of 65° and traveling for one hour, indicate the amount of time and what general direction to take should you want to go for a swim.

A. 250° for 1:45 minutes; Southeast for 45 minutes

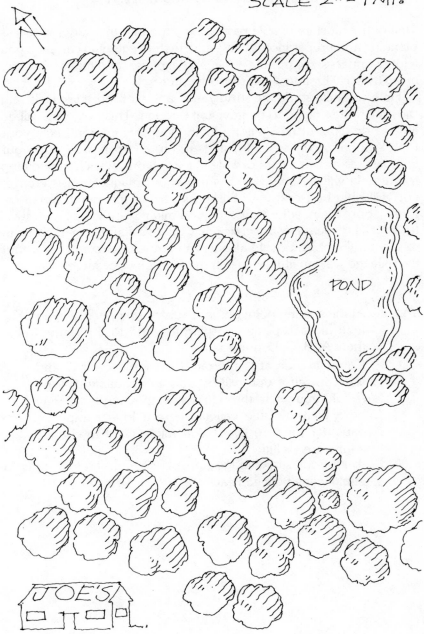

SCALE 2" = 1 MI.

POND

JOE'S

Planning the Cross-country Trip

One of the most enjoyable parts of any trip into the wilderness is its planning and preparation. A little care in the beginning can save you a lot of unnecessary trouble, time, and expense, and make your stay away from civilization a pleasant adventure.

First, carefully study the survey map and familiarize yourself with the area you're going to be traveling through. This way, you will be able to do all your navigation plotting long before you begin your trip. You will need a small ruler, a very sharp pencil, and your compass, as well as a comfortable place to work. A kitchen or dining room table will do fine. Don't worry about magnetic interference, you will only be using your compass card at this point. For now, forget about the needle. However, you might want to buy a protractor which is a clear plastic semicircle with 180 degrees marked off in raised numbers. You could also use a marine or aircraft plotter, but the mileage scale might not match the ones on your survey map.

Plotting Your Course

STEP 1   At the starting point on your survey map, pencil in an "X," then at each place you plan to visit, do the same. Label them A, B, C, D, and so on.

STEP 2   Carefully look at the terrain between each "X" and ask yourself if you will be able to negotiate it. Why should you wade through a swamp when there may be a pleasant little valley where a lonely trapper's daughter (or son) lives? You might want to change your course a little.

STEP 3   Take your straightedge and pencil and carefully draw a straight line between each "X."

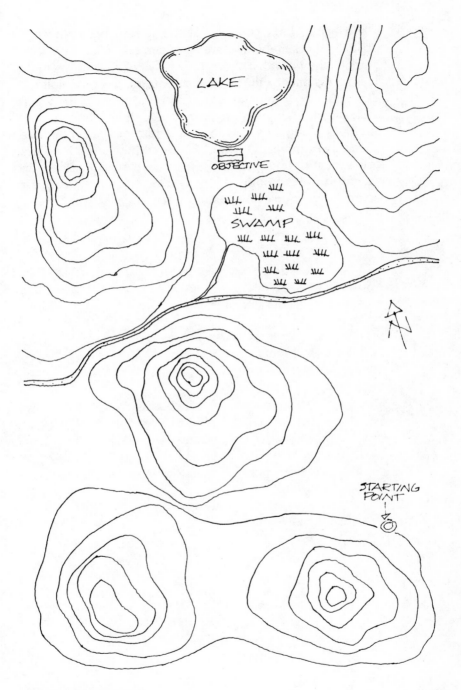

LAKE

OBJECTIVE

SWAMP

STARTING
POINT

STEP 4 Once again, look carefully at the terrain between each objective for suitable features you can use as checkpoints. Mark each one with a checkmark.

STEP 5 This is the most difficult and important of your plotting. You must now find the true compass readings between each direction change on your course. If you have a protractor or plotter, it's just a matter of placing the center hole of the instrument over the "X" or somewhere along the course line you've drawn. Then, make sure it's lined up true North and South. When you've done this, read the degree your course line passes under.

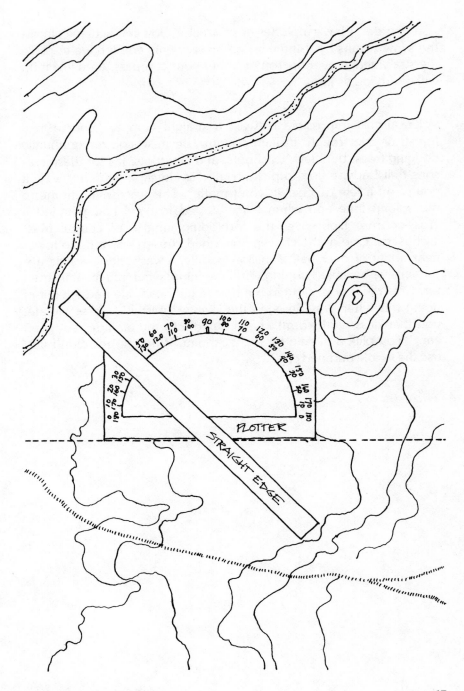

If you don't have a plotter or protractor, you can achieve almost the same results by using your compasss, only you'll have to place the straightedge over the top or under your compass, then line it up with your course line.

It's almost impossible to walk a straight compass course in a forest, or over rough, broken country, because you're continually dodging trees, boulders, washouts, and whatnots. It's for these reasons that I advise you to pick prominent checkpoints. That way, if you're off a few degrees it won't matter. This was driven home to me a long time ago when I first started to fly. I had planned a cross-country flight over the forbidding jungles of central Massachusetts. One of the checkpoints I had chosen was a radio tower near a city of over half a million people. I was getting a little apprehensive because I couldn't find the thing, when my flight instructor, Crash McLoop, clouted me upside the head. He had a habit of doing this when I made even the slightest mistake. "You ingrate, you thankless earthworm!" he shouted into my already reddened ear. "You pick a needle for a checkpoint. Why the hell didn't you use the whole damned city?"

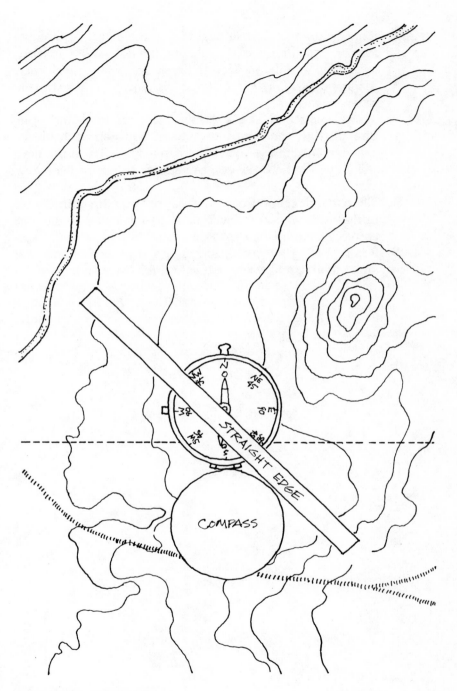

STEP 6   Convert the true course headings to magnetic. At the bottom of your survey map you'll find the degree of variation. (See chapter 4 if you need to brush up.) Now, pencil each magnetic heading along its course line together with its reverse heading.

STEP 7   Using the scales at the bottom of your map and your straightedge, measure the distance between each objective and checkpoint and pencil it in along each course line. When you're finished, you can add up the mileage of your trip.

STEP 8   Choose a direction from the area that you are going to be in that will get you to civilization as quickly as possible in case of an emergency.

STEP 9   After plotting a course, always go over everything one more time to make sure you didn't make a mistake.

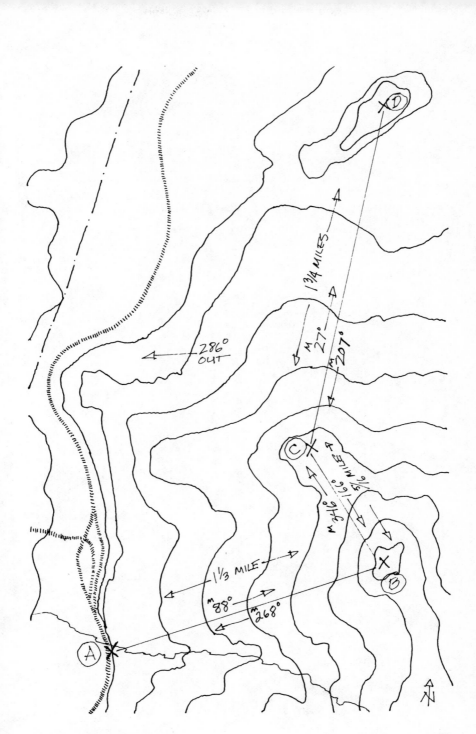

286°
OUT

1¾ MILES

M 27°

M 207°

3/6 MILE

M 346°
166°

1⅓ MILE

M 88°

M 268°

N

CHAPTER
6
Safety in the Field

Preparation

Safety should be the key element in any planned venture away from civilization. Whenever possible, keep the odds in your favor.

Always let friends know where you're going to be and how long you'll be gone. Give them copies of your survey map with your navigation plot circled. They may not understand it, but a forest ranger or park warden will be able to use it to track you down. After considering the time factor and giving yourself plenty of leeway, say an extra day, you may give your friends a deadline, and tell them to call the authorities if they haven't heard from you by that time. It's always a good idea to stop by the nearest ranger or police station and tell them your plans. They may have information that could be helpful and save you trouble. Perhaps the streams are swollen, or some bigshot from the city has bought a tract of land and posted it.

Choose your equipment carefully. An overnight trip will not require a 50-pound pack. Always take into consideration the weather and the time of year when picking out clothes. I personally prefer to travel light, as I find a heavy pack more of a burden and not worth some of the goodies it carries.

Make an equipment, clothing, and supplies checklist and use it. On the following page is a list of items you may want to consider taking before leaving on a cross-country trip. In making up your own list, you should think twice about some of the things you pick. Is that battery-operated, computerized, portable makeup kit and hair dryer really that necessary? You also may want to leave behind some of the extra food you were going to bring. Perhaps you could instead hunt for fresh game, and gather edible plants that grow in the wild.

Equipment List

1. Spare compass (always a good idea), and don't forget to tie your first one to your belt.
2. Extra map (maybe not for yourself, but for another member of your party).
3. Large and small plastic bags (to keep things dry in wet weather). You can use the small ones for your navigation

equipment and valuables, such as your wallet, notebook, and maps. Use the large ones (garbage bag size) for your pack and sleeping bag. Maybe you'll have to ford a stream or swim a river.

4. Wooden, waterproof matches (you can make your own by melting some wax and dipping the tips in it).
5. An 8-foot square sheet of plastic. It weighs little and can be used for a spare tent or a groundsheet, or even a large raincoat for everyone to get under in case of a downpour.
6. Knives. (I recommend a standard hunting knife with a 3–5-inch blade, and a small pocket knife or Swiss army type clasp knife with all the extra doodads.)
7. If you wear eyeglasses, always take a spare pair along.
8. A bright red or blaze orange hat or jacket if you're going to be in the forest during hunting season. We want you to come home behind the wheel and not across the fender.
9. A hunting license if you're going to shoot game.
10. A single shot twelve-gauge shotgun with twenty rounds of assorted shot from number 7½ to a couple of rifle slugs. If you're going to be primarily exploring and traveling and only wish to shoot to feed yourself and friends, this combination can't be beat. It's easy to carry, and with the variety of ammunition you can stop anything from a humming bird to godzilla.
11. Fifteen feet of ½-inch nylon rope. (This has a thousand uses, from holding up your tent to dragging out that big buck you just shot.)
12. Insect repellant.
13. Snake bite kit, should you be in an area where the little beasties thrive.
14. Portable citizen band walkie talkies for each member of your group.
15. Obviously you will want to consider such matters as flashlights, tents, sleeping bags, first-aid kits, and even extra food in case the hunting and fishing turn sour.

As you can see, there is an almost endless variety of useful things that you can take along, and you'll have to decide which of these apply in your case. But, remember this—someone has to carry it all.

Lost

Let's assume that you went and you got yourself well and truly lost. Now you can throw up your hands to the heavens and issue forth that time-honored battle cry that rings like a clarion call across the length and breadth of our nation each summer and fall. WHERE THE HELL AM I? If you're in a group, there is a little variation of the call that's much too lewd to print here. Perhaps you've heard it on occasion from your boating friends. It has something to do with a tribe of lost Indians.

Well, now you've really got things to worry about. Let's say it's getting dark and the sky is overcast and nothing looks familiar. Perhaps someday they will find the dust of your bones after the lions, tigers, bears, gorillas, and Big Foot get through with you, let alone the tree that stalks by night and the eggplant that ate Chicago. If none of these monsters brings about your end, there is one that will, and he can be the most dangerous enemy you will ever have in the wilderness, if you don't keep him under control. That enemy is yourself. Your own imagination can do more damage than any animal you'll ever run into. (In most cases, when a wild animal gets your scent, it sets out to establish a new land speed record in the opposite direction.)

The first thing to do when you realize that you're lost is to admit it. Don't start walking fast or running; that won't solve the problem. Sit down and cool it for a few minutes. There are some important things to take into consideration. While you're sitting there regaining your composure, listen very carefully. Perhaps you can hear the sound of traffic on a distant highway or a farmer's barking dog or some man-made sound you can get a bearing on. Remember, if you're in hill country, sound can appear to come from several different directions at once. Be sure you have the right one before setting out. If you don't hear anything, or even if you do, climb a tree or the nearest hill. Maybe you will recognize a landmark or see where the sound is coming from.

Let's say you haven't heard or seen anything. Now check your watch and estimate how much time you have before dark. You're going to need that time to find a nice comfortable spot to spend the night. If that sounds frightening, just cool it; you'll find your way in

Safety in the Field

the morning. There's no big deal to spending a night in the woods.

Take the weather into consideration. What is it doing? Is it cold? Maybe it's started to snow. If so, you must keep as warm and dry as possible. I'm sure by now you have realized that the weather is the one real enemy you have in a situation like this. Try to find yourself a thick stand of pine or fir trees away from the wind, preferably on a gradual sloping hillside. This will help keep you dry and afford drainage should it rain. Now start gathering every stick of dry wood in sight and begin stockpiling it beside your campsite. If the wood on the ground is damp, use dead limbs from standing trees. One tip to remember should you be in an area where birch trees are available—birch bark will burn even if it's wet. You may want to gather some to help you start your fire. What if it's a warm, dry night? Build a fire anyway. It will give you something to do during the night, and if people are trying to locate you, it will help.

In case you have lost your compass, find your westerly direction by getting a look at last light or sunset. You may have to climb a tree to do it, and when you have done so, draw a compass on the ground. You know by facing West your right hand will be pointing North. Should you hear gunshots or sound signals during the night, you'll know what direction they came from. In the morning, first light will give you your easterly direction.

If you've been hunting, wait until almost dark before trying to signal your friends. You wouldn't want to shoot too early as they might think you were shooting at game. The standard rule is to fire three shots at well-spaced intervals, then listen. (Save one of your empty cartridges. It will make a wonderful whistle that can be heard for almost half a mile. To use it, press the open end hard against your lower lip and blow.) I personally don't recommend walking through a forest on a dark night. It's a good way to break a leg or fall into an empty well. Nevertheless, if the weather is clear and you can see the moon or stars, and the country you're in is not too rugged, go ahead—just slow your pace and be careful. A little later on in this chapter, I'll show you how to find your direction by the stars.

Just for a moment now, let's put the shoe on the other foot. Instead of being lost, suppose you are searching for a lost friend. If you have an idea where your lost friend is and you have a vehicle that can get into the area, go as close as possible to where you think he is and blow your horn three times—well-placed blasts every 2 minutes—and listen for a return signal. Another instrument you can use to attract attention just short of waking the dead, is a chain saw. Nothing in this world makes a racket quite like this machine. During the day the sound is almost intolerable, and at night it's obscene. If you're within 10 square miles of the lost person he will hear it. Just remember, he may be a long way off, so keep up a steady racket, which will enable him to home in on you. Should you be at a campsite and a member of your party doesn't make it back before dark, make a big fire, being careful not to let it spread, of course, and then make a lot of noise. Gunshots, pots, pans, whistles, anything at all will be helpful. You may have to keep up this racket half the night, but most of the time it does the trick. Never leave a campsite to look for a lost friend at night. At best, you can only travel a few miles an hour. Sound, on the other hand, travels about 700 miles an hour. Besides, you could wind up getting lost or hurt yourself. If you haven't located the lost person within a reasonable amount of time—let's say 2 to 5 hours—you should contact the authorities.

Now, getting back to the party of the first part. Comes the dawn's early light, you'll be ready to move. If you have a compass and a map, finding your position won't pose too much of a problem. First, get to high ground and line your map to the true North. Then locate your last known position on your map and estimate approximately how much time you spent traveling from that position. I assume you already know how far you usually travel in a given span of time. For example, let's say you travel 2 miles an hour and you walked 2 hours before you realized you were lost. Now you know you are at least 4 miles from that last known position. By using the distance scale on your map, draw a 4-mile circle around your last position. Carefully study the lay of the land and see if any of it matches up with anything within the circle. If so, the rest is easy. Simply draw a line from your present position to one on your original course line. Measure the distance and pencil in checkpoints. Figure out the magnetic heading, estimate the time of travel, and off you go.

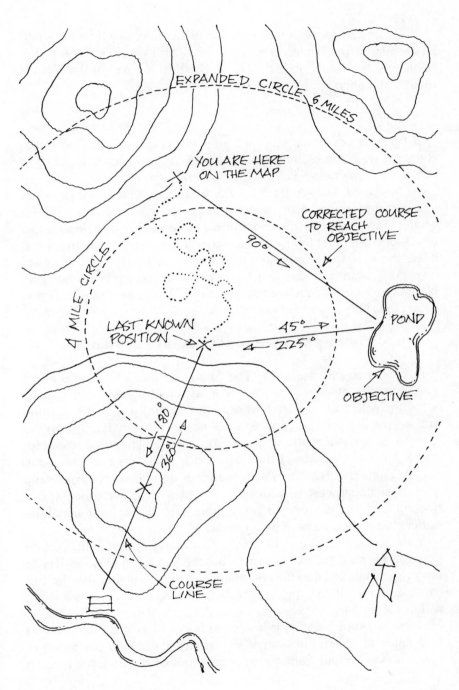

EXPANDED CIRCLE 6 MILES

YOU ARE HERE ON THE MAP

CORRECTED COURSE TO REACH OBJECTIVE

90°

4 MILE CIRCLE

POND

LAST KNOWN POSITION

45°
225°

OBJECTIVE

180°

360°

COURSE LINE

N

Now, let's suppose you are unable to locate yourself on the map. First, enlarge the circle by another hour and carefully look at the additional territory—no luck. Okay, climb to the top of the highest nearby elevation.

If by now you can't pinpoint yourself, you don't belong there. Remember, in the plotting phase of your trip you picked a direction out of the wilderness. Well, now is the time to use it.

At this point, let's go back a little. If you can't find your position, can you find water? Most streams, lakes, ponds, and rivers will be on the map. Suppose you come upon a stream, but you don't know which one it is. Just follow it downstream. If it junctions with others, it will show on the map, and you'll have your position. If not, it will eventually lead you out, but I recommend you stick to your pre-planned get-back-to-civilization direction. That stream may take you a long way before you get out.

Getting Out Without Compass or Map

You have two choices here. The first is to stay where you are if you're sure someone has started a search for you, or if you or someone with you is injured. Should this be the case, find a clearing and keep a fire going, a nice big smokey one. If there is snow on the ground, stamp out a huge SOS. If you have a big enough clearing, make it immense—about the size of a football field will do quite nicely. Then line the letters with branches and leaves. A fixed-wing aircraft at its slowest is traveling around a mile a minute and it doesn't take long for one to get by you. The bigger your signal the better chance you have of being spotted.

Your second choice is to move. Get going at first light. Maybe you don't have a compass or map, but the sun is just as good. Try to remember the direction you planned to get you out and use the sun as your guide. If the day is cloudy and overcast or it's snowing, without something to give you a direction, you'll just walk in a circle. My best recommendation is keep heading for low ground until you find water. No matter how small the stream, it will lead you to larger ones. If you should happen on a cart trail or grown-over logging

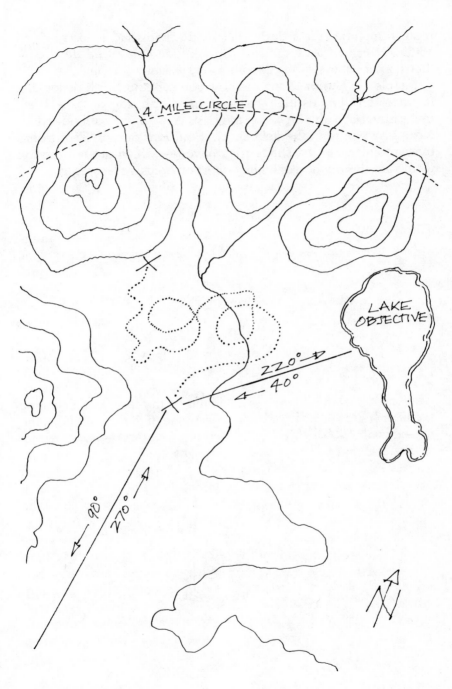

4 MILE CIRCLE

LAKE OBJECTIVE

220°
40°

90°
270°

road, remember the vehicle that made them had to come from somewhere, so follow the trail. Should you come to a dead end, then it's certain that going the other way will take you out.

People are always telling me how you can find North by looking for moss and fungus that grows on the North side of trees. Well, that's true, but it also grows on the East, West, and South sides, too. Next time you're in the field check it out for yourself. Tree trunks that are always in the shade may have growth all around them. I would use this method of finding direction only as a last resort.

POLE STAR

Safety in the Field

Traveling at Night Without a Compass

As previously stated, you can get about at night without your compass, provided the weather is clear and the terrain you're in is not too rugged. There is one exception to this that can be quite helpful. Lights from towns, villages, and highways will reflect on a low overcast and can be seen for miles. You may be able to guide on these reflections until you find civilization or establish a direction line to them that you can follow in the morning.

The other way is to do what man has done for centuries. Simply follow the stars. As a charter boat captain, one of the things I enjoy most is taking anglers game fishing at night, especially if the sea is calm and there is no overcast. Once I am out of the harbor and clear of all obstacles, I point the bow toward a familiar star and go fishing. My vessel, the *Sea Witch,* has all the best electronic navigation equipment aboard. But, when possible, I'll chase a star to my destination. This method may not sound scientific, but it sure puts a little romance back into running a boat.

The following illustration of the night sky will show you how to find the North Star at different times of the year. Once you've located it, you have found a fixed position directly over the North Pole. Through the night the heavens appear to rotate around this star as the Earth revolves. You must remember this. Should you be guiding on a star near the horizon, keep checking your direction of travel from the North Star. You may want to change the star you're guiding on after a time. Another thing to remember is that the North Star isn't the biggest one in the sky. You'll have to do a little looking before you recognize it.

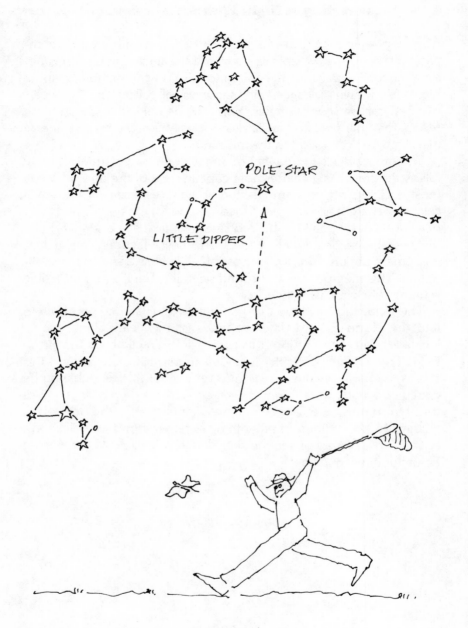

POLE STAR

LITTLE DIPPER

Spring

Safety in the Field

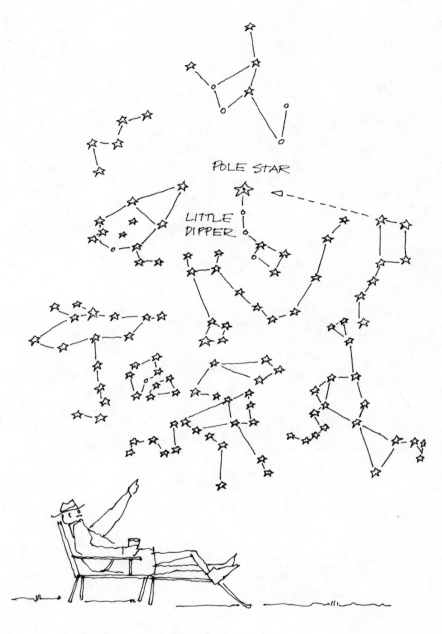

POLE STAR

LITTLE
DIPPER

Summer

Safety in the Field

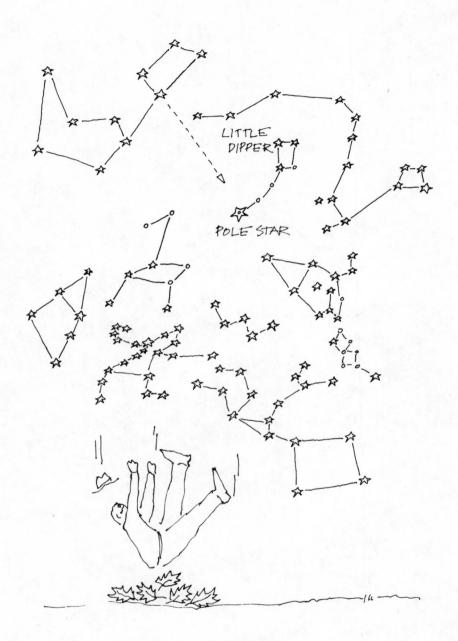

Fall

Safety in the Field

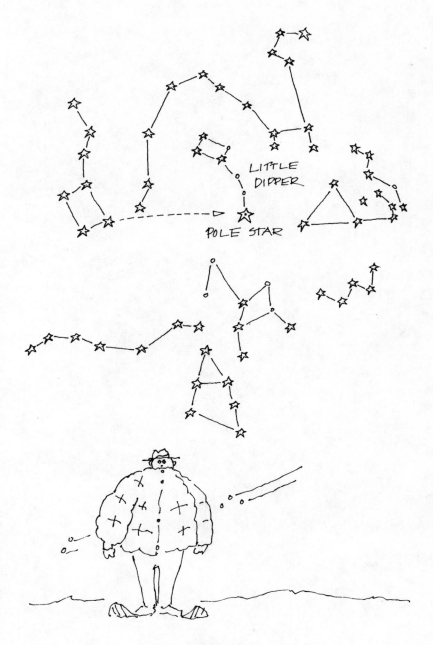

Winter

7

Navigation for the Boatman

The subject of marine navigation is a detailed science with many facets. The purpose of the following chapter is only to acquaint you with a few fundamentals of piloting and is not to be considered a complete text in any sense of the word. However, the beginning boatman will find the information helpful in maintaining safe navigation of his vessel and in pointing the way to more advanced navigation techniques.

Each year a tragic story is retold along America's waterways, especially along the Atlantic coast. Hundreds of people set out in their boats and are never seen alive again. There are also many thousands who become lost or involved in marine-related accidents. It is my personal contention, after almost 20 years at sea, that 75 percent of these accidents were waiting to happen. The prime ingredients of these accidents and tragedies are the words "neglect" and "forget" and sometimes plain old stupidity in its most basic form.

The story behind each fatality and mishap usually sounds something like this: "I neglected to learn how to use a compass." "I forgot to fix the bilge pump." "I didn't bother to check the weather." "I didn't slow down in the fog." "I didn't replace." "I didn't repair." "I didn't check." "I didn't think." And there is the greatest undoer of all time which, in a sense, is stupidity in another state—"I was drunk."

It never ceases to amaze me how people sometimes go out of their way to get killed. The following story is a good example. Several years ago in the early spring, three men decided to make a trip from an upper Cape harbor to Provincetown, a distance of nearly 30 miles. Their vessel was an 18-foot fiberglass runabout with a 125-horsepower engine. The weather forecast was for a Northeast storm with winds of 25 knots, gusting to 45. They had a full tank of fuel, and the capacity of the tank was 6 gallons. The storm had set in before they left, but do you think this stopped these brave souls from their destiny? Not so. Off they went into the teeth of a Northeast storm in an 18-foot boat with 6 gallons of fuel. I know this is a little hard to believe, but it gets even worse. A trawler captain whose vessel was tied to the dock saw them loading up and tried to warn them, but he was rewarded for his efforts with what appeared to be half of a V for victory salute. Well, to make a long story short, one body was found and the other two were never seen again. The Coast Guard and the newspapers reported it as an accident—I suppose for lack of another word. I, however, have chosen one that seems to fit this incident and several I know of like it. *Stupidcide*. Simple, unmeditated stupidcide. Their chance of survival was about the same as if they dressed in fuzzy brown suits with antlers and ran through the woods during the opening day of the deer season.

Safe boating is a combination of many factors:

1. Good equipment.
2. Careful planning.
3. Accurate information.
4. Thorough inspection.
5. Knowing the rules of the road.
6. Knowing your vessel's limitations.
7. Knowing your own limitations.
8. Just plain common sense.

Always keep the odds in your favor and your trip on the water will be rewarding and enjoyable.

One recommendation that I can make to the beginning boatman is to join a power squadron of your local Coast Guard auxiliary, or at least enroll in one of the many courses they offer. You'll learn a lot of useful things and have a lot of fun, too.

The Nautical Chart

Understanding the nautical chart will require a little effort on your part, but in comparison to a geological survey map, you'll find it delightfully easy to use. One of the first things you'll notice is that in convenient places about the chart are printed compass roses. The outer circle gives you true headings and the inner one magnetic headings. Each rose is printed with the variation indication on its center.

To plot a course, all you'll need is a straightedge and a pair of parallel rulers. Simply draw your course line on the chart. Now,

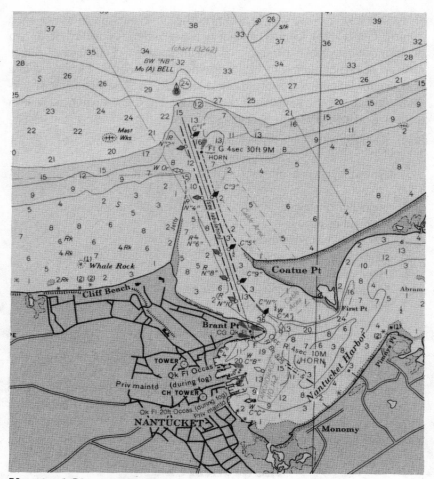

Nautical Chart of Harbor

place the outer edge of the parallel ruler along the course line and swing the other edge over the center of the nearest compass rose. You can now read the magnetic as well as the true heading. You won't have to worry about figuring the variation because the chartmaker has done it for you.

Nautical charts come in four different types, beginning with the harbor chart which shows a detailed view of a small area. Every boatman should have one of his home port and familiarize himself with it.

The second on the list is the coastal chart. This type of chart covers a somewhat larger area showing bays, harbor entrance sounds, and all navigation aids. They are ideal for the beginning boatman as they will enable him to navigate safely near shore.

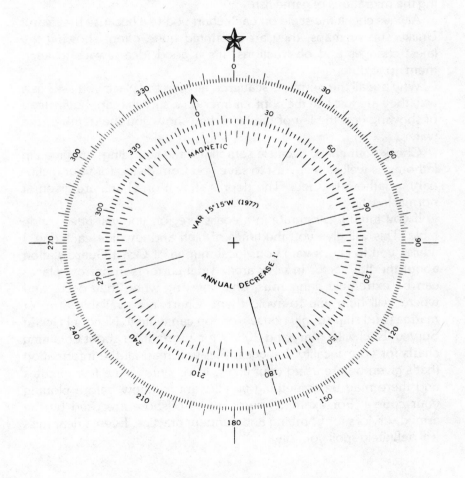

A typical compass rose.

Next is the general chart which is used primarily for coast-wise navigation, where a vessel may still be able to see shore but remain far enough away to avoid coastal dangers. Offshore fishermen and weekend yachtsmen find these charts ideal for their purpose.

Another chart which is of little use to the average boatman is the sailing chart. It covers a huge area and is used by ships to obtain their position before making shore. I use this type of chart aboard my aircraft when fish spotting. They are excellent for use in following the migrations of game fish.

Always check the scale on each chart you use because they vary. Unlike survey maps, they are reprinted quite often, showing the latest changes and obstructions. It's a good idea always to keep them up to date.

Why are all the numbers scattered all over the place you ask? In a way they are just like the contour lines on a survey map, but instead of showing you the lay of the land they show you the depth of the water.

Check your chart, because sometimes the soundings are given in fathoms as well as feet. Just to save you from diving for your dictionary, a fathom is 6 feet. The depths shown on charts are given at normal low tide.

If you intend to operate in a coastal region you will need a tide table. This will give you the times of high and low tide each day. I advise you to check with your local marina or Coast Guard station about the tide factor in your area. Tidal currents in narrow places can be extremely dangerous, and knowing when they occur and where, will help you to avoid them. Charts are available at most marinas and ship supply houses, or you can write to National Ocean Survey, Rockville, Maryland 20852 for information about obtaining charts for your locality. I suggest that you read all the information that's given before using your chart. It will only take a few minutes and there may be something you'll want to know before plotting your course. For example, some areas offshore are used by the armed services for bombing and gunnery practice. Even a near miss will definitely spoil your day.

Aids to Navigation

Any person who drives a motor vehicle in the United States can get into it and drive to a city that is unfamiliar to him, over roads that he has never traveled before, just by following road signs. These are aids to navigation. The boatman does pretty much the same thing when he navigates in coastal waters. He uses a combination of man-made and natural landmarks to tell him where he is. On a highway you may encounter signs that tell you there's danger ahead or to avoid a certain area.

On the water, you have the same tools. A lighthouse is one. Understanding and recognizing aids to navigation is of paramount importance to the boatman. On the following pages, you can see the basic buoy system of the United States. You should pay particular attention to the ones that apply to your area. One helpful exercise you can do after obtaining charts of your area is to match up as many symbols as you can with the following ones. (In these illustrations, those buoys marked "port" are kept to the left, those marked "starboard" to the right, of the channel when heading *upstream* ([or from a larger body of water to a smaller one elsewhere]). Obviously you must keep them on the other side when going the other way.)

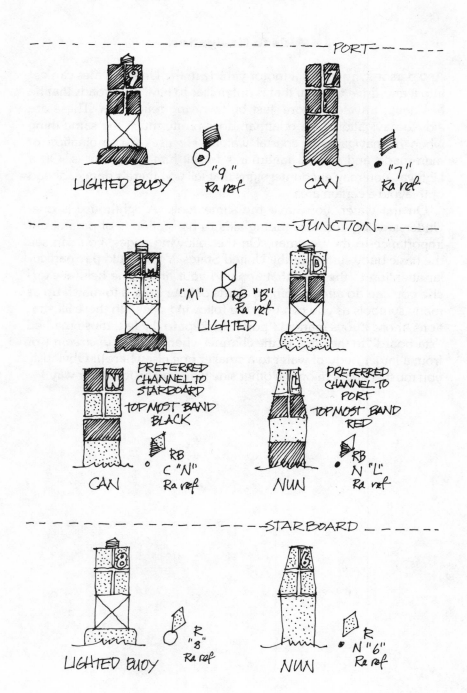

Navigation for the Boatman

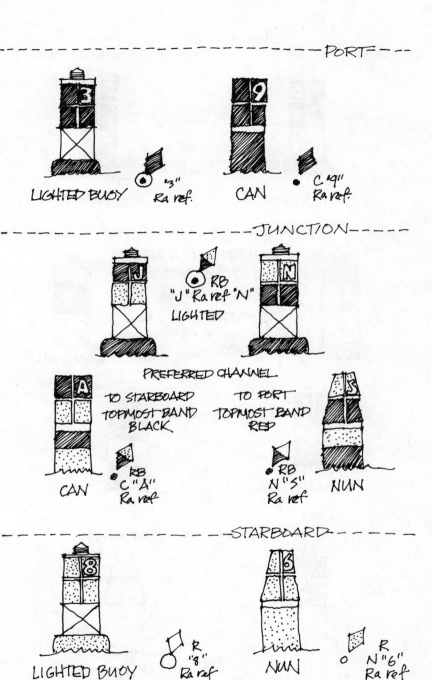

PORT

LIGHTED BUOY "3" Ra ref.

CAN C "9" Ra ref.

JUNCTION

RB
"J" Ra ref "N"
LIGHTED

PREFERRED CHANNEL

CAN

TO STARBOARD
TOPMOST BAND
BLACK

RB
C "A"
Ra ref

TO PORT
TOPMOST BAND
RED

RB
N "S"
Ra ref

NUN

STARBOARD

LIGHTED BUOY R "8" Ra ref

NUN R N "6" Ra ref

- -PORT- - - - - - - - - - -

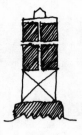

LIGHTED BUOY

CAN

- -JUNCTION- - - - -

PREFERRED CHANNEL
TO STARBOARD
TOPMOST BAND BLACK

PREFERRED CHANNEL
TO PORT
TOPMOST BAND RED

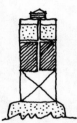

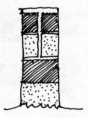

CAN

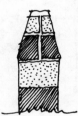

NUN

- -STARBOARD- - - - -

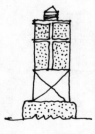

LIGHTED BUOY

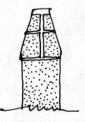

NUN

Navigation for the Boatman

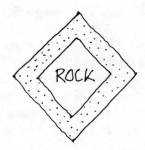

DIAMOND SHAPE WARNS OF DANGER!

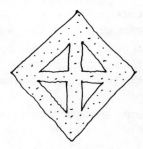

DIAMOND SHAPE WITH CROSS MEANS BOATS KEEP OUT!

CIRCLE MARKS A CONTROLLED AREA.

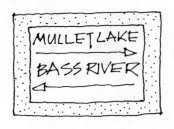

SQUARE OR RECTANGLE GIVES INFORMATION, NAMES, ACTIVITIES.

Plotting on the Nautical Chart—Steps 1 through 5

Earlier we showed you how to plot a course on the survey map. If you're going to be using a course you have plotted and followed on numerous occasions, after a while all the landmarks and even the vegetation along your way will become familiar to you, so that eventually you won't need your chart or even your compass to follow it. As long as you can see, you'll be able to stay on your trail. The boatman, on the other hand, must be able to follow his trail even though his visibility may be limited to a few yards and there are no identification marks between each reference point.

When plotting your navigation courses for your area of operation, you must assume that someday you'll get caught in a low-visibility situation. Fog, heavy rain, and thick haze can easily be navigated in provided you have done your homework and planned for these inconveniences beforehand.

Usually when I get to this subject during a discussion in the classroom, someone, and there always is one, sticks up his bony little hand and says, "So just use your radar." I answer this by telling him that we will pretend he left the cover off during maintenance and a sea gull dive-bombed it, and now because of his negligence the wretched thing won't work. At this point, every navigation tool in the book gets mentioned—from fathometers, radio direction finders, and loran sets to an occasional big ball of string. I conveniently put them all in the hock shop or leave them on dock, and we're left only with the chart and the compass.

To make this information as clear as possible, let's assume that you're going to be operating your vessel from a small sheltered harbor that empties into a large body of water.

STEP 1   With a straightedge, draw your course line from your harbor to the harbor entrance buoy. See following illustration.

Navigation for the Boatman

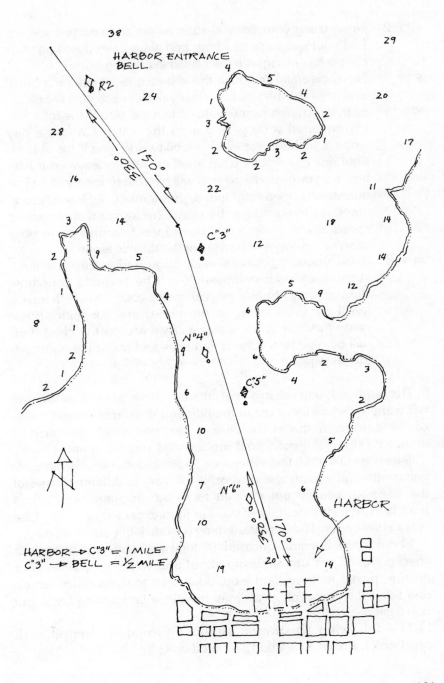

38

29

HARBOR ENTRANCE
BELL

R2

24

4

5

4

20

1

2

3

3

2

2

1

28

17

2

3

2

16

11

22

18

14

3

14

5

14

C"3"

12

2

5

9

14

1

5

9

12

8

1

4

6

2

2

1

N"4"

6

2

3

9

C"5"

4

6

2

1

6

5

10

2

7

N"6"

6

HARBOR

10

5

N

19

20

14

HARBOR → C"3" = 1 MILE
C"3" → BELL = ½ MILE

STEP 2   Now, using your parallel ruler as we showed you earlier, find your magnetic headings and write them down on your course line along with their reverse readings.

STEP 3   Next, carefully measure the distance between each buoy and write the information clearly under each course line.

STEP 4   At this point the best way to obtain the rest of the information required is by getting it on the water. Choose a day when you have excellent visibility and you'll be able to sight one checkpoint from another. As you leave your harbor, set your throttle so you will be able to maintain a slow but steady operating speed. Remember, in low visibility you have to go slow to be safe. Check your tachometer or speedometer or both and record this information on your chart or notebook. Then leave the throttle alone.

STEP 5   Time yourself between each buoy and record the time. Also check your compass. You'll be pointing your bow right at these buoys as you make your run. If there's a small compass error, or the buoys are not quite in the same position in the water as they are on the chart, you will be able to see the differences and make the appropriate changes.

Remember, if you are in a coastal area where tide is a factor, you will want to record the stage of the tide and the direction and speed of the current. If this is the case, when you reach the channel entrance buoy, turn your boat around and run the return course. This way you'll find the difference in time between checkpoints going with and against the current. It will vary at different stages of the tide, but usually not enough to cause any great amount of trouble. You'll either get there quicker than expected or it may take you a little longer. The important thing is to stick to your compass.

Should you become encased in total fog and you miss your checkpoints, don't run aimlessly about and waste fuel. Drop your anchor, post a lookout, and blow your horn to warn other vessels and listen for their reply. You may be a little late getting back, but you'll get back.

The following illustration shows information compiled in notebook form for navigation in limited visibility.

Marine Navigation Form

Check Point	Mag. Course		Distance	Time	Speed
	To	Return			
1. HARBOR	C"1"	350°/170°	1 MILE	15 MIN.	4 KTS.
2. C"1"	BELL	330°/150°	½ MILE	7½ MIN.	4 KTS.
3.		/			
4.		/			
5.		/			
6.		/			
7.		/			
8.		/			
9.		/			
10.		/			

Tachometer Setting 11 RPM

Speedometer Reading 4 KTS.

E T A   12:00 P.M.

A T A   12:05 P.M.

Tide   HIGH

Current ½ KT.

Notes:

Emergency Radio Channels CH 9 CB
VHF CH 16

Weather Channel 162.55

Electronic Navigation Aids

The rest of this chapter will be devoted to basic description and use of some of the pieces of equipment that we left at the pawnshop a few pages back.

Depth Finders

Other than a good radio or a good first mate, a depth finder is one of the most valuable pieces of gear you can have aboard. The machine works by transmitting an ultrasonic signal toward the bottom and measuring the time it takes for the signal to return. These machines come in two parts. The indicator, which is usually mounted near the helmsman (that's the boat driver), and the transducer, which is externally mounted on the bottom of the boat. Depth finders also come in portable units for use in small outboards and runabouts. The transducer, then, is usually attached to the stern or side of the vessel.

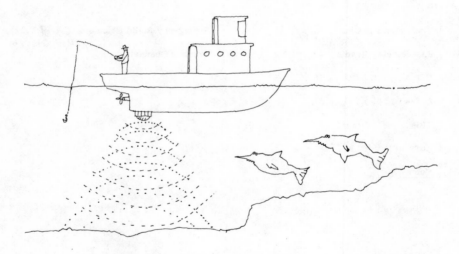

Radio Direction Finder

This device gives you bearings to shore-based radio transmitters. The instrument consists of a radio receiver with several operating bands. A 360-degree circular grid is usually affixed to the top of the case with a tunable loop antenna in its middle. The use of the

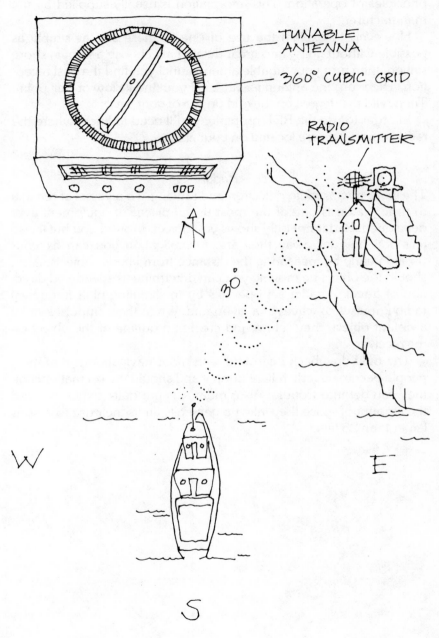

R.D.F.

TUNABLE ANTENNA

360° CUBIC GRID

RADIO TRANSMITTER

N

30°

W

E

S

instrument requires a little practice and a lot of understanding of its principles of operation. This information is usually supplied by the manufacturer.

However, to explain the use of one of these sets as simply as possible without going into great detail: First choose a known shore station, then turn your tunable antenna until you find the best reception. Then turn the antenna away until you find its low or null point. Then read the degree on the grid on top of your set.

In order to use the RDF properly, you'll need to know where the radio transmitters are located on your chart.

Radar

The word means radio detection and ranging. To a vessel at sea in a thick fog radar is one of the most useful pieces of equipment ever developed. Radar not only shows you objects around you but it also tells you how far away they are. In navigation you can fix your position early by measuring the distance from known objects. Also, should the object be moving you can determine its speed and direction of travel. A radar set operates by transmitting high frequency radio impulses or waves at a given rate. When these impulses strike a distant object, they return and create an outline of the object on the receiver.

The only drawback I can find with radar navigation is that most people become overly reliant upon it and should the set malfunction they can get into trouble. Also, radar sets are quite expensive and the amount of space they take up generally limits their use to vessels larger than 25 feet.

Navigation for the Boatman

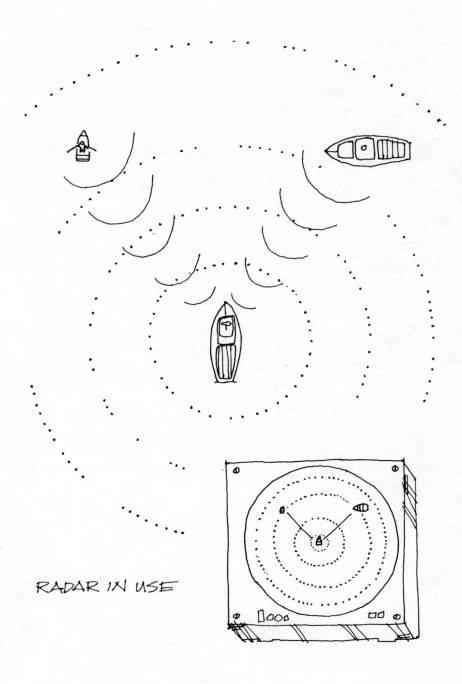

RADAR IN USE

Further Reading

For those interested in a complete text on small boat navigation, I recommend Charles F. Chapman's *Piloting Seamanship and Small Boat Handling* (published by Hearst Books, New York, and revised from time to time). This is one of the most comprehensive and best written books ever printed on the subject.

Other recommended books on advanced navigation and seamanship are:

Dunlap, G.D. & Shufeldt, Capt. H.H., *Dutton's Navigation and Piloting,* 12th Edition. Annapolis, Naval Institute Press, 1972.

Von Dorn, William J., *Oceanography and Seamanship.* New York, Dodd Mead, 1974.

Navigation Notebook

This book contains three types of forms that will help you in your basic exercises and on cross-country trips and voyages. Also, you will find the equipment and checklist helpful in remembering what to bring and inspect before leaving.

Basic Exercises Form

Objective: Departing from:

Distance: Magnetic course _____ Degrees

                    Return course _____ Degrees

Departure time: Arrival time:

Check-point: Check-point:

Check-point: Check-point:

Compass variation: True course:

Speed:

Notes:

Objective: Departing from:

Distance: Magnetic course _____ Degrees

                    Return course _____ Degrees

Departure time: Arrival time:

Check-point: Check-point:

Check-point: Check-point:

Compass variation: True course:

Speed:

Notes:

Cross-Country Navigation Form

Objective: Departing from:
Overall distance: Departing time:
Mag. Course: Compass variation:
Checkpoints: Distance:
                              Time:

1.
2.
3.
4.
5.
6.
7.
8.
9.
10.

Notes: *Total time:*

Direct course out of wilderness _____ to _____.

Equipment List

1.	13.	25.
2.	14.	26.
3.	15.	27.
4.	16.	28.
5.	17.	29.
6.	18.	30.
7.	19.	31.
8.	20.	32.
9.	21.	33.
10.	22.	34.
11.	23.	35.
12.	24.	36.

Notes:

Nearest Police: PHONE: LOCATION:

Ranger Station: PHONE: LOCATION:

Car parked at:

Car description:

Plate No.:

In case of emergency phone:

Marine Navigation Form

CHECK-POINT TO RETURN	MAG. COURSE	DISTANCE	TIME	SPEED
1.	!			
2.	!			
3.	!			
4.	!			
5.	!			
6.	!			
7.	!			
8.	!			
9.	!			
10.	!			

Tachometer Setting: Emergency Radio Channels:

Speedometer Reading: Weather Channel:
E T A:
A T A:
Tide:
Current:

Notes:

Boatman's Checklist

1. Fuel
2. Spare fuel
3. Oil
4. Spare oil
5. Fresh water
6. Battery
7. Spare battery
8. Jumper cables
9. Stuffing box
10. Hose clamps
11. Transmission oil
12. Water pump drive belts
13. Spare spark plugs
14. Shire pins
15. Spare prop
16. Bilge
17. Blower
18. Bilge pump
19. Switches
20. Fuel filters
21. Steering
22. Lights
23. Horn
24. Radio
25. Depth finder
26. Life jackets
27. First-aid kit
28. Ring buoy with line
29. Flares
30. Flashlight
31. Towing line
32. Bucket
33. Binoculars
34. Charts
35. Spare compass
36. Paddle
37. Sunglasses
38. Tools
39. Fire extinguishers
40. Copy of rules of road

INDEX

Aviation maps, 21

Boating navigation, 90–107
  aids to, 95–99
  electronic aids, 104–107
    depth finders, 104
    radar, 106–107
    radio detection finders, 104–10
  form for limited visibility situation,
    102–103
  nautical charts, 91–94
    compass roses, 91–92
    depth figures, 94
    types of, 92–93
  plotting on nautical charts,
    100–102
  tide tables, 94
Boating safety, 90–91

Coastal charts, 21
Common sense, 4, 51
Compass error, 24–25
Compass variation, 20–24
  rule for, 22
Compasses,
  gyro, 15
  lensatic, 12
  magnetic, 10–11, 20–25, 28–48
  marine, 12–13
Cross-country navigation, 51–70
  dead reckoning, 57–62
  planning a trip, 64–70
    plotting the course, 64–70

Dead reckoning, 57–62
Degrees, 8
Direction arrow, 12
Direction circle, 5–8

Gyro compasses, 15

Homing, 11

Isogonic lines, 21

Lensatic compasses, 12

Magnetic bearings, 28
Magnetic compasses, 10–11
  compass error, 24–25
  use of, in field, 28–48
  variation of, 20–24
Magnetic interference, 24–25
Magnetized (magnetic) needle,
  10–11
Marine compasses, 12, 13

Navigation,
  aids to, 3–4
  aids to water travel, 95–99,
    104–107
  for the boatman, 90–107
  cross-country, 51–70
  example of, 2–3
  exercises,
    Around the Block, 30–33
    Estimating a Direction, 46–48
    Navigating Away from
      Civilization, 37–44
    There and Back, 28–29
    Treasure Map, 34
North, importance of, 10
North Pole,
  magnetic, 20
  true, 20

Reference points, 3

Safety in the field, 74−87
   care in choice of equipment, 74−75
      equipment list, 74−75
   inform friends of trip particulars, 74
   lost in the woods, 74−83
      getting out without compass or
         map, 80−82
      locating water, 80
      searching for another person,
         77−78
      traveling by the stars, 83−87
      you are lost, 76−77, 78−83
Speed of travel, 30

Sun's position, value of knowing,
   30−33

Time involvement, 30, 44
Topo(graphical) maps. *See* U.S.
      Geological Survey maps

U.S. Geological Survey maps, 21,
   51−57
   accuracy of, 55
   contour lines, 52−55
   distance scales on, 56
   indications to north on, 56−57